THE WORLD'S STUPIDEST Husbands

THE WORLD'S STUPIDEST Husbands

Diana Briscoe

First published in Great Britain in 2005 by
Michael O'Mara Books Limited
9 Lion Yard
Tremadoc Road
London SW4 7NQ

A CIP catalogue record for this book is available from the British Library

ISBN 1-84317-168-6

1 3 5 7 9 10 8 6 4 2

Designed and typeset by
K DESIGN, Winscombe, Somerset

www.mombooks.com

Printed and bound in Britain
by Cox and Wyman Ltd, Reading, Berks

Introduction

'Behind every successful man is a woman, behind her is his wife.'

Groucho Marx

Groucho probably didn't mean it that way, but most women would agree that a man needs more than just one woman around if he is to achieve success. Perhaps the reason why the stupid husbands that you will find in this book achieved their depths of stupidity was because they only had their (overworked, and much-put-upon) wife to back them up.

Of course, most husbands do not reach their most mind-bogglingly stupid moments at home.

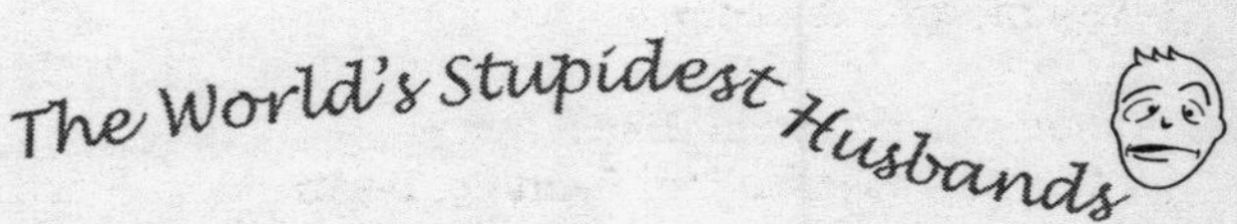

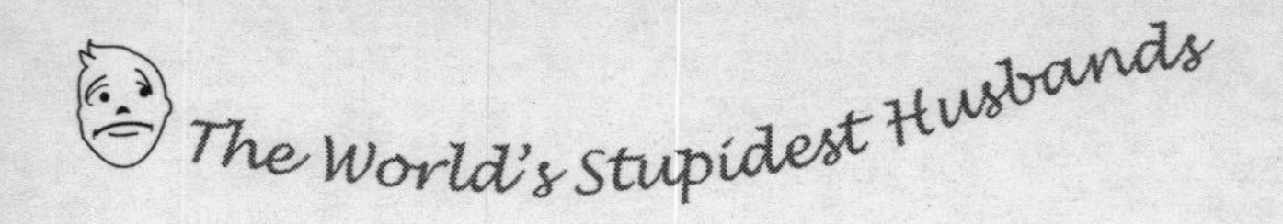

It's when they are released into the community, far away from the guiding hand of the women who watch over them, that things start to go seriously pear-shaped.

From the husband who lost his steering wheel to the one who killed his friend with a cigarette butt, not to mention the public pronouncements and published words of men whom you would have thought *really* could not be that stupid, this is a cornucopia of stories, jokes, quotes and recorded incidents of husbands reaching the ultimate in stupidity.

Of course, if your husband has topped them, we'd love to hear about it . . .

What's She Reading?

Three men were standing at a bar discussing coincidences. The first man said, 'My wife was reading *A Tale of Two Cities* and she gave birth to twins.'

'That's funny,' the second man remarked, 'my wife was reading *The Three Musketeers* and she then gave birth to triplets.'

The third man shouted, 'Good God, I have to go home now!' When asked what the problem was, he exclaimed, 'When I left the house, my wife was reading "Ali Baba and the Forty Thieves!"'

Who Was It?

John returns from a four-week business trip to New York and finds out that his wife Sadie has been unfaithful during his time away.

'Who was it?' he shouts at Sadie. 'Was it that bastard Sam?'

'No,' replies Sadie, 'no, it wasn't Sam.'

'So was it Charlie, that degenerate old man?'

'No, it certainly wasn't him.'

'Then it must have been that simpleton Bill.'

'No, it wasn't Bill either,' replies Sadie.

John is now very angry. 'What's the matter?' he yells. 'Are none of my friends good enough for you?'

Ask And You Shall Receive

One weekend, three husbands went off on a hike. They unexpectedly came upon a large raging, violent river. They needed to get to the other side, but had no idea of how to do so.

The first man prayed to God, saying, 'Please, God, give me the strength to cross this river.'

Wham! God gave him big arms and strong legs, and he was able to swim across the river in about two hours, but only after almost drowning a couple of times.

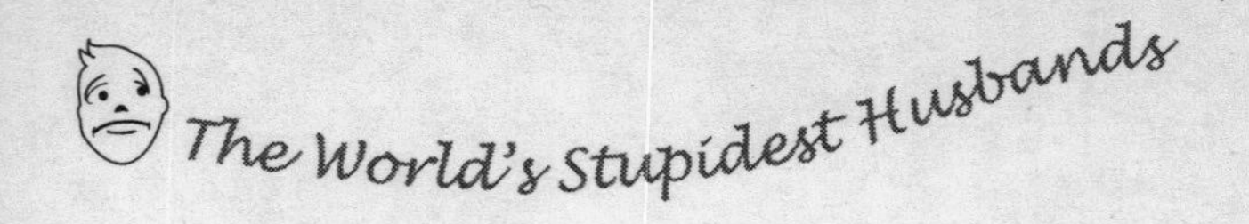

Seeing this, the second man prayed to God, saying, 'Please, God, give me the strength . . . and the tools to cross this river.'

Wham! God gave him a boat and he was able to row across the river in about an hour, but only after almost capsizing the boat a couple of times.

The third man had seen how this worked out for the other two, so he also prayed to God saying, 'Please, God, give me the strength and the tools . . . and the intelligence . . . to cross this river.'

And wham! God turned him into a woman. She looked at the map, hiked upstream a couple of hundred yards, then walked across the bridge.

The Warning

David, a senior citizen, was driving round the M25 towards Heathrow when his mobile phone rang.

When he answered it, he heard his wife urgently warning him, 'David, I just heard on the news that there's a car going the wrong way down the M25. So please be careful!'

'Hell,' said David, 'It's not just one . . . there are dozens of them!'

Confessions

The night before their wedding, Alf and Betty were sharing confidences.

Alf said, 'You must know something before we get married. I am a fanatic golfer. I eat, sleep and drink golf. Golf is my whole life. After we are married, I'll try for some balance but I doubt whether I'll succeed. Just understand – you're marrying a golf addict.'

'I can live with that,' said Betty, 'now I'll tell you my secret – I'm a hooker.'

'A hooker?' Alf repeated. 'I can live with that. Next time, keep your head down and your left arm straight, then swing through the ball . . .'

In The Thunderbox

A stupid husband in Blacksville, West Virginia, was occupying a portable toilet when he decided to light a cigarette to pass the time while nature did its stuff.

According to a spokeswoman for the local ambulance service, the methane in the Portaloo 'didn't take too kindly' to the lit cigarette. The loo exploded in a fireball.

The man was able to drive himself to a nearby health centre, from where he was transferred by ambulance to hospital. The hospital refused to reveal whether the man's injuries were serious enough to ensure he could not pass on his stupidity to the next generation.

Easy Rider?

A 47-year-old sheriff of Albany County, Wyoming, was 'born to be wild' – he owned a Harley-Davidson, which he habitually rode without a helmet, despite his wife's worries about the risks. In 2003, he went to a motorcycle rally in South Dakota, riding with a couple of friends.

Along the way, he decided he wanted a photograph to commemorate the trip. As they rode along at 65 mph, he got out his camera and turned around to snap a picture of the rider behind him.

As he did so, the sheriff's motorcycle drifted right and headed for a telephone pole. He lost control of the bike trying to straighten it up, and was thrown off. He broke his skull, four ribs, a shoulder blade, and had other head injuries and road rash, but amazingly he survived his stupidity. His camera was not so lucky!

Recycling Maniac

A stupid Croatian husband was killed while trying to open a hand grenade with a chainsaw.

He was trying to recycle the explosive to make fireworks for the New Year's holiday.

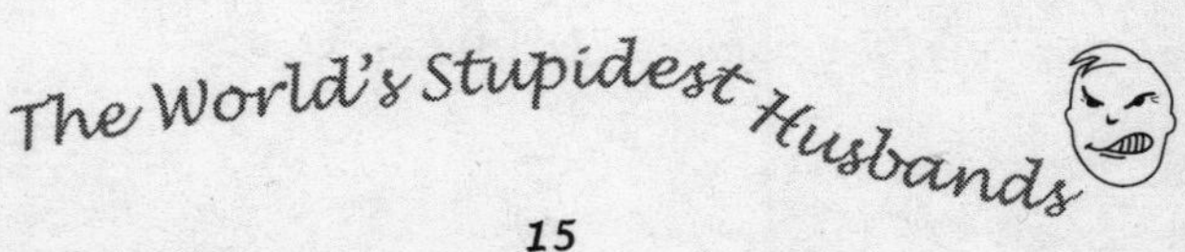

Was His Name St Peter?

A man in Texas was drowned when he was swept away by high water as he walked across a spillway.

He was trying to convince his wife that it was safe to drive across . . .

Sealed Away

A farmer from São Paulo, Brazil, needed to remove a swarm of bees from his orange tree. He didn't know exactly how to proceed, but he knew the swarm should be smoked to pacify it, and he knew that bees sting. So he put on a pair of gloves, protected his head by sealing a plastic bag tightly around his neck, lit a torch, and went off to deal with the bees.

His worried wife went to look for him a few hours later, and found him dead. However, it wasn't the bees that killed him. The plastic bag had protected him from smoke, stings – and oxygen! He had forgotten to make any breathing holes in the bag.

'I Told You . . .'

An angry husband returned home one night to find his wife in bed with a naked man.

'What are you doing?' he shouted.

To which his wife said to her lover, 'There! I told you he was stupid.'

Whether Question

A businessman's trip has been cancelled unexpectedly, so he is at home with his wife, who seems a little nervous. They go to bed, but at about midnight the phone rings. Before the wife can get it, the man rolls over and answers it.

'Hello? What? How the hell should I know . . . I live in Birmingham!'

He slams the phone down, and rolls over, grumbling.

His wife asks, somewhat nervously, 'Who was that, dear?'

'I don't know,' the man replied. 'Some idiot wanted to know whether the coast was clear.'

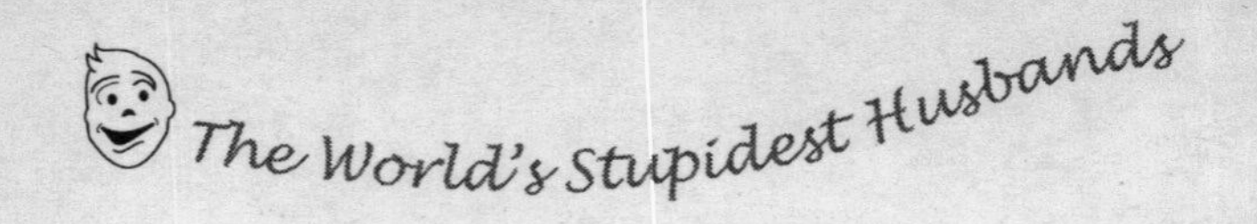

Have you heard about the stupid husband on the underground?

The power went off and he was trapped on an escalator for two hours.

Old Chinese Proverb

Foolish man give wife grand piano.
Wise man give wife upright organ.

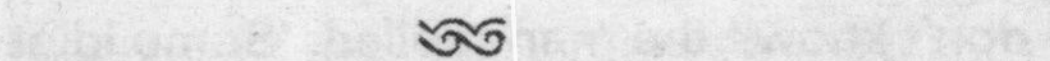

Once a wife told her husband that they
use alligators to make shoes.

He shook his head and said,
'What will they teach them to do next?'

Blood-y stupid

A stupid husband was ordered by the court to take a paternity test.

'Were you the father?' asked one of his friends.

'They'll never find out,' he said. 'They took the sample from my finger.'

Towel Technique

Fred was unable to satisfy his wife. He had tried loads of techniques, but just couldn't give her an orgasm. Finally he went to his best friend and asked for advice. His friend told him not to worry because he knew a method that was 100 per cent successful.

He said, 'Hire a well-hung young stud to stand near your bed and wave a huge towel over both of you while you are having sex. This way your wife will be stimulated and have an orgasm.'

Fred hired the stud, but all his efforts were in vain. He went back to his friend and told him what happened. So his friend suggested that they switch places.

'Why don't you wave the towel while the stud does the job in bed?' said the friend.

Poor Fred agreed, saying he would do anything to satisfy his wife. He hired the same guy again and this time they traded positions. Naturally, the wife had a divine orgasm.

The husband leaned over to the young stud and said, 'You see! That's how you wave the fucking towel!'

My Husband Is SOOOO Stupid . . .

. . . when I asked him to buy me a colour TV, he asked, 'Which colour?'

. . . when you stand next to him, you can hear the ocean.

. . . when asked on an application, 'Sex?', he wrote, 'M, F, and sometimes Wednesday too'.

. . . the Oxford Dictionary had to change the definition of 'dumb'.

My Husband Is SOOOO Stupid . . .

. . . they had to burn his school down just to get him out of primary school.

. . . you have to dig for his IQ.

. . . when he read on his job application not to write below the dotted line, he wrote 'OK'.

. . . when our baby was born, he looked at the umbilical cord and said, 'Wow, it comes with cable too!'

Cursed by the Crystals

The state of Chihuahua in Mexico is home to two hot caverns containing the largest natural crystals known to man. Some of the clear selenite crystals are more than 20 feet long. Over a thousand feet below the surfacce of the earth, it is rumoured that anyone attempting to plunder their riches is visited by a curse.

A man recently tried to steal one of the magnificent crystals from the roof, and might have succeeded – if he hadn't stood directly beneath it while chopping it free.

He was pinned beneath the stalactite when it fell, and died of heat exhaustion in the 42 °C (108 °F) temperature of the cave.

Always Check the Chamber . . .

A California man shot himself dead while explaining gun safety to his wife. He placed a .45-calibre pistol, which he thought was unloaded, under his chin and pulled the trigger.

His wife told police that the incident had occurred after her complaints about her husband's seventy guns prompted him to demonstrate their safety.

Stupid Sports Moments – USA

Men, I want you just thinking of one word all season. One word and one word only: Super Bowl.

BILL PETERSON, NFL FOOTBALL COACH

The word 'genius' isn't applicable in football. A genius is a guy like Norman Einstein.

JOE THEISMAN, NFL FOOTBALL QUARTERBACK AND SPORTS ANALYST

Not only is he ambidextrous, but he can throw with either hand.

DUFFY DAUGHERTY, NFL FOOTBALL COACH AND SPORTS ANALYST

Cigarettes Can Kill You!

Two stupid husbands in New Jersey, USA, were having a 'boys' night out', when one challenged the other to shoot him with cigarette butts 'to see what it would feel like'.

His friend obligingly loaded an antique rifle with cigarette butts, placing black powder behind the butts to make sure they left the barrel of the gun. He then shot his friend from a distance of 7 feet.

The projectiles penetrated the rib cage of the 31-year-old who had issued the challenge, and he died of three cigarette butts to the heart.

Pull, Then Pull

A 34-year-old man had been involved in an argument at a billiards room in Calgary, Canada. Later, he came back to settle the score.

According to witnesses, as he pulled a small-calibre handgun from his waistband, it went off and hit him in the groin. The man, described by his wife as 'distraught', was taken to a hospital for treatment.

'His injuries weren't life-threatening, but I would suggest they were life-altering,' said Calgary Police Inspector John Middleton-Hope.

Calling Cards

In South Africa, a stupid thief left his parole card in a pair of jeans he had discarded after changing into stolen clothes in the house that he had just burgled.

He snatched jewellery, silverware and electronics from the house, but was quickly caught using the information he had so carelessly provided. When fingerprints found at the scene of the crime matched those on his parole card, he was duly sent back to jail.

Mr Pooter Takes Up DIY

April 25
In consequence of Brickwell telling me his wife was working wonders with the new Pinkford's enamel paint, I am determined to try it.

I bought two tins of red on my way home. I hastened through tea, went into the garden and painted some flowerpots. I called out Carrie, who said: 'You've always got some newfangled craze;' but she was obliged to admit that the flower-pots looked remarkably well.

Went upstairs into the servant's bedroom and painted her washstand, towel-horse, and chest of drawers. To my mind it was an extraordinary improvement, but as an example of the ignorance of the lower classes in the matter of taste, our servant, Sarah, on seeing them, evinced no sign of pleasure, but merely said 'she thought they looked very well as they was before.'

April 26
Got some more red enamel paint (red, to my mind, being the best colour), and painted the coal-scuttle, and the backs of our SHAKSPEARE, the binding of which had almost worn out.

April 27
Painted the bath red, and was delighted with the result. Sorry to say Carrie was not, in fact we had a few words about it. She said I ought to have consulted her, and she had never heard of such a thing as a bath being painted red. I replied: 'It's merely a matter of taste.'

FROM *THE DIARY OF A NOBODY*
GEORGE AND WEEDON GROSSMITH

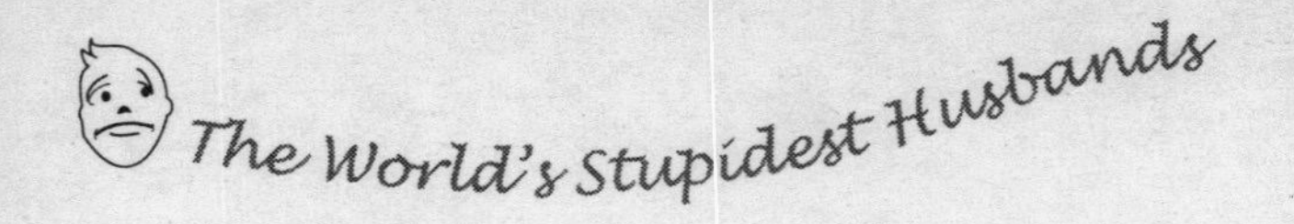

Too Correct?

George Traugott Breeckow, a German-born American, was executed as a spy by firing squad in London on 26 October 1915. Although he was not the first German spy to be executed during the First World War, Mr Breeckow certainly made it as easy as possible for the British to catch him.

His job was to observe troop movements in Britain and then send the details to his contact in German-occupied Rotterdam. However, British intelligence was naturally inquisitive about letters to addresses in enemy territory and started opening Mr Breeckow's mail. The contents were compromising enough to alert them that there was a spy operating in the country somewhere.

They did not have to wait long to find out where exactly he was based. Mr Breeckow obviously suspected that his letters were not being delivered and must have decided that this was because he was not completing the envelopes properly. The next time he posted his report, he wrote his name and address on the back of the envelope . . .

Stupid Things Stupid Men Say

When a woman becomes a scholar there is usually something wrong with her sexual organs.

FRIEDRICH WILHELM NIETZSCHE,
GERMAN PHILOSOPHER, POET AND CRITIC

The Blessed One said, 'Amrapali, the mind of a woman is easily disturbed and misled. She yields to her desires and surrenders to jealousy more easily than a man. Therefore it is more difficult for a woman to follow the Noble Path.'

THE TEACHINGS OF BUDDHA, FIFTH CENTURY BC

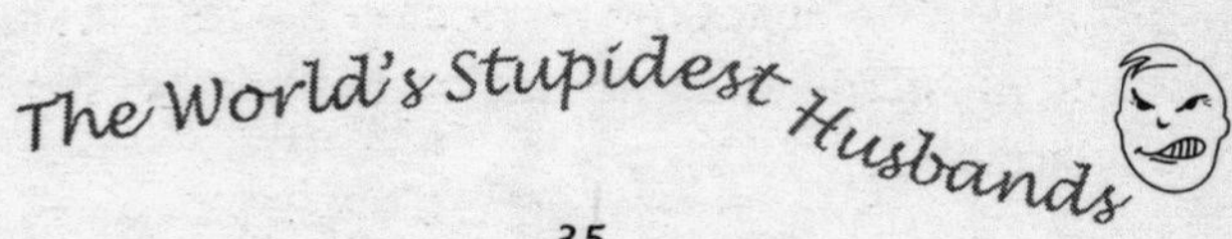

Stupid Things Stupid Men Say

Women ruin music. If the ladies are ill-favoured, the men do not want to play next to them, and if they are well-favoured, they can't.

SIR THOMAS BEECHAM,
BRITISH CONDUCTOR

Man does not exist for the sake of woman, but woman exists for the sake of man and hence there shall be this difference, that a man shall love his wife, but never be subject to her, but the wife shall honour and fear the man.

MARTIN LUTHER, GERMAN RELIGIOUS REFORMER,
FROM *VINDICATION OF MARRIED LIFE*

Curiosity Kills . . .

Our office has a paper towel dispenser in the kitchen. It holds a roll of paper towels without a cardboard tube in the centre, and towels are pulled from a hole in the bottom. It is also refilled from the bottom. To prevent the roll from falling out before the base is closed, it is fitted with a 'non-return device' – a set of plastic flaps that hinge up but not down.

One of our programmers was very, very bored. He wandered into the kitchen to make himself a coffee and, as he waited for the kettle to boil, he noticed that the towel dispenser was empty with its base hanging open.

Suddenly, he felt a urge to see what the towel dispenser looked like from the inside. His head fitted inside fairly well, but he stood on tiptoe for a even better view. As he did so, the non-return device 'non-returned' right under his chin.

How long can you stand on your tiptoes? His colleagues heard thrashing, choking noises coming from the kitchen and found him dangling by the throat from the towel dispenser. Fortunately, they were able to release him without permanent damage, although his wife did ask some pointed questions about the marks on his neck that evening. Sadly, no one had a camera handy.

It Takes All Sorts!

A 40-year-old male came in to our hospital complaining of abdominal pain and rectal bleeding. He claimed to be unaware of any reason for such symptoms. But during his examination, the physician discovered a coat hanger protruding from the patient's rectum.

When questioned, the man admitted he had inflicted this injury upon himself. Earlier that night, while his wife was at work, he was 'pleasuring himself' when he had an urge to push an uncooked egg into his anus. In an attack of panic when he lost it 'up there', he tried to fish the egg out with the crooked end of a coat hanger. But the coat hanger became snagged!

He decided that perhaps the vibration from a ride on his motorbike would dislodge the whole mess

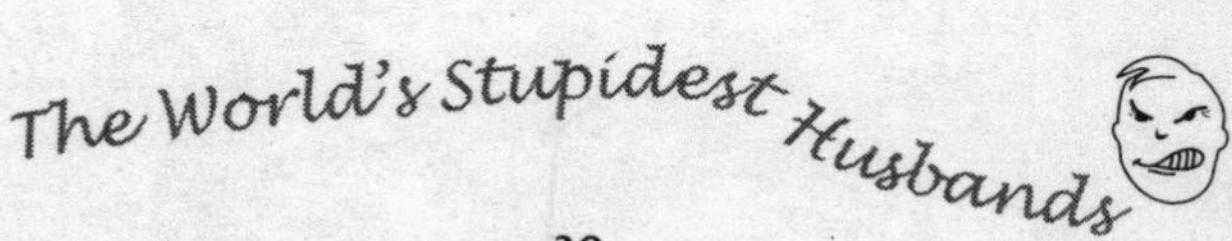

from his arse. Finally, when this did not work and unable to stand the growing pain, he rode his motorcycle to our Accident and Emergency. A surgeon removed the coat hanger, and performed an emergency bowel resection.

An hour later, his wife arrived. Minutes later, she stormed out of the room and demanded to be told what had happened. I told her she should ask her husband. She said he claimed that he didn't know, and that the medical staff wouldn't tell him anything. She was politely, but firmly, instructed to speak to the man's doctor. Poor woman!

I met my husband at a dance and he was the best-looking man on the floor . . . I can see him now, lying there.

WIFE: Shall I cut your sandwich into two or four pieces?

HUSBAND: Better make it two – I couldn't manage four.

My husband's at home recovering
from a freak accident – he was suddenly
struck by a thought.

After twenty years of marriage,
I'm finally developing an attachment
for my husband –
it fits over his mouth.

Every Action Has A Reaction

A casual acquaintance related this adventure suffered by her husband in Michigan, USA.

A high wind had blown a huge tree branch across the electricity lines behind their house, and the line was close to breaking. Her husband decided to remove the branch from the wire himself.

Enlisting the aid of a friend, he balanced the ladder against the taut wire, climbed up, started the chainsaw, and carefully began cutting. He had almost managed to free the branch, and only one more cut was needed when the whole branch fell to the ground, releasing the wire. Of course, the wire sprang back to its original position.

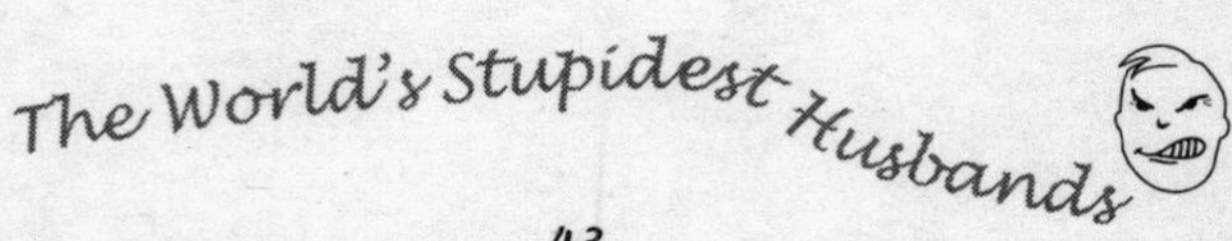

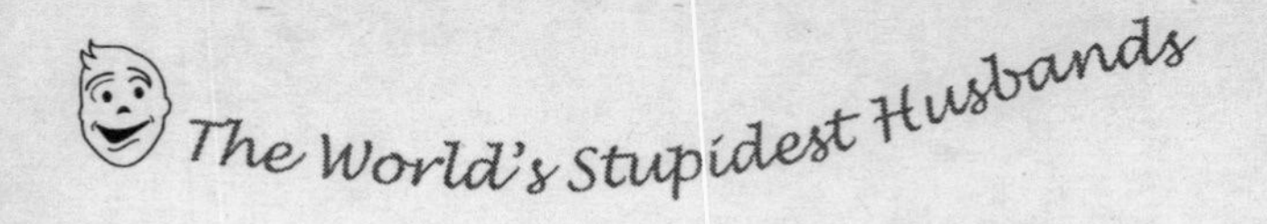

The force lifted the ladder several feet into the air, along with its chainsaw-wielding occupant. The ladder slipped away, and Joe fell against the wire, knocking the chainsaw into his face, and missing his carotid artery by mere inches.

He managed to throw the chainsaw away from himself, preventing further injury from that source, but then hit the ground extremely hard. Fortunately, her husband survived with a only broken leg and some stitches. She was also adamant that next time they would wait for a professional!

Gravity In Action

Two young firemen were moving one of their families out of a third-floor flat to a house around the corner during the 1960s. The two friends discovered that the kitchen appliances were extremely heavy, so they decided to lower them down from the flat roof using a rope.

One of the firemen was over 6 feet tall, and weighed 18 stone, so he acted as anchorman. He stood well back from the edge of the roof with a rope tied around his waist. The other stood at the edge of the roof and controlled the speed of the rope with his hands.

The first item they lowered was a refrigerator. Both men braced their feet against the load, but despite their combined efforts, the refrigerator's speed of descent increased, and the rope began

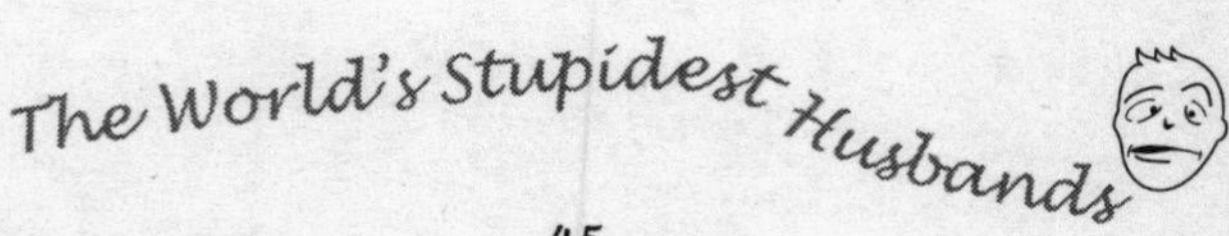

to burn the controller's hands. Finally he had to release it.

He turned to see his friend racing across the roof towards him – and the edge – flat out, screaming curses and clawing at the stacks as he tried to halt his mad dash.

Had either of them thought to measure the rope? Miraculously it was longer than the height of the building. The refrigerator hit the ground, before the anchorman hit the edge (just!).

The rest of the items were carried down the three flights of stairs.

'Blow In This, Sir'

A stupid husband was trying to convince his wife that he was sober enough to drive. So he drove to the police station in his pickup truck, parked illegally, and demanded a breathalyzer test. He failed and was taken into custody.

'Basically,' an amused police sergeant explained, 'his wife won the argument.'

Go Out With A Bang

In Khabarovsk in the far east of Russia, a man who had threatened to 'deal with' his wife and her lover blew himself up with a home-made bomb.

The bomb exploded when the husband tried to attach it to the door of the lovers' supposedly secret apartment.

A Senior Moment

Sharon and Graham went out for a drive in their large Mercedes. Graham was driving and Sharon was in the front passenger seat. After a few minutes, they came to some traffic lights but, although the lights were clearly at red, Graham drove the car across the junction.

Sharon says to herself, 'I must be losing it. I could have sworn we just went through a red light.'

A few minutes later, they come to another set of lights and again they go through red, this time narrowly missing a car driving across them. Although Sharon was sure the light was at red, she's convinced she's losing it, and is now very nervous.

At the next junction, the light again shows red and, as before, the car goes across without slowing.

So Sharon turns to Graham and says, 'Hey, did you know that you just jumped three red lights in a row? What on earth are you doing – are you trying to kill us?'

Graham turns to Sharon and replies, 'Blimey – am I driving?!'

How Could She Have Guessed?

My cousin Bob owned one of the biggest and fastest-growing businesses in London, a furniture store.

I convinced him that he needed to take a trip to Italy to check out the merchandise himself and because he was still single, he could check out all the hot Italian women, and maybe get lucky.

As Bob was checking into a hotel, he met a beautiful young lady. She only spoke Italian and he only spoke English, so neither understood a word the other spoke.

He took out a pencil and a notebook and drew a picture of a taxi. She smiled, nodded her head

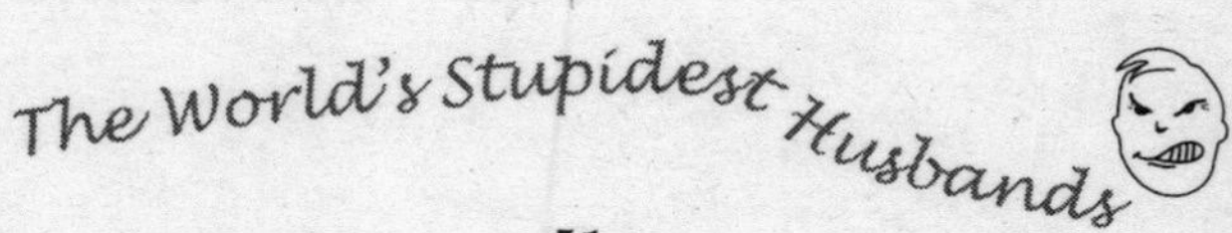

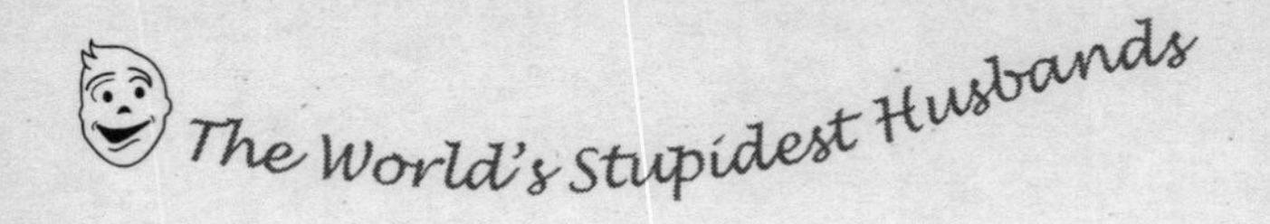

and they went for a ride in the park. Later, he drew a picture of a table in a restaurant with a question mark and she nodded, so they went to dinner.

After dinner he sketched two dancers and she was delighted. They went to several nightclubs, drank champagne, danced and had a glorious evening. It had gotten quite late when she motioned for the pencil and drew a picture of a four-poster bed.

Bob was dumbfounded, and to this day remarks to me that he's never been able to understand how she knew he was in the furniture business.

Up For It!

Thomas, an elderly man, goes to a brothel and tells the madam that he would like a beautiful, young lady for the night because his wife died last week.

The madam looks at him quickly and is rather puzzled. So she asks him, 'How old are you?'

'Why,' replies Thomas, 'I'm 98-years-old today.'

'Ninety-eight!' the madam exclaims. 'Don't you realize you've had it?'

'Oh,' Thomas says, 'in that case, how much do I owe you?'

Misunderstanding

A young rabbi met with his board of directors to beg them to buy a new chandelier for the synagogue. Arguing and pleading for over an hour with the board, he eventually sat down believing he had failed.

Then suddenly, the president of the board said, 'Why are we wasting here time talking? My wife's promised me salmon tonight! First of all, a chandelier . . . why, we haven't got anyone who could even spell it! Second, we haven't got anyone who could even play it. And lastly, what we really need in the synagogue is more light!'

What Came Of Being A Cheapskate

Adam was bored in the Garden of Eden, so he says to God, 'Lord, I have a problem.'
'So what is your problem, Adam?' replies God.
'Lord, I know that you created me and gave me all this wonderful food and put me in this beautiful garden, but I'm just not happy.'
'Why is that, Adam?', God asked.
'Lord, you created this world for me and you gave me all these friendly animals to be with, but I am still lonely.'
'OK, Adam,' said God, I have the perfect solution – I shall create a woman for you.'
'What is a "woman", Lord?'
'A "woman" will be such an intelligent creature that she will know what you want before you ask for it. She will be so sensitive and caring that she

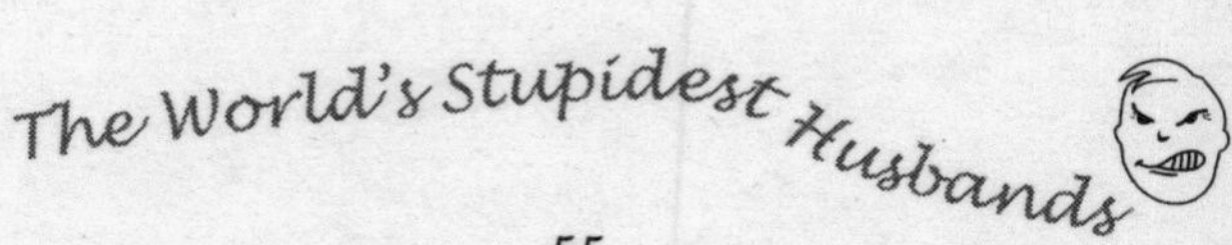

will know your every mood and how to make you happy. Her beauty will be the equal of anything on earth. She will care for your every need and desire. She will be the ideal companion,' says the voice from Heaven.

'This woman sounds great to me, Lord.'

'She will be, take my word for it, but she comes at a price, Adam.'

'So how much will she cost me, Lord?' Adam asks.

'She will cost you your left arm, your right foot, one eye, one ear and your right testicle.'

Adam thinks about this for a good sixty minutes, working out all the pros and cons of having such a woman for company, but especially the cost to him.

Finally Adam says, 'OK, Lord, what kind of woman can I get for just one rib?'

The rest, as they say, is history.

The Book Buyer

Did you hear about my brother-in-law, Frank, who was sexually inexperienced?

One day, he was in a bookshop and saw a book that he thought might help called *How to Hug*.

It was only when he started to read his new book that Frank realized it was Volume 7 of the *Encyclopedia Britannica*.

The Astronaut

Morris, the Jewish astronaut, was asked why he was packing a tie for his space mission.

He replied, 'My mother said that when I do a space walk, I should look nice.'

Later on, Morris desperately radioed Mission Control from orbit, 'I must make an emergency landing right now!'

'Why?' asked Mission Control, 'what's gone wrong?'

'My wife called and she wants to be picked up from the hairdresser.'

Back To Front

80-year-old Paddy is very upset indeed when he calls the Garda. He shouts, 'Help me! I'm in the centre of Cork and my car's been broken into. The thief has stolen the radio, the steering wheel, the gear lever and the pedals. What should I do?'

The dispatcher says to him, 'Stay calm, sir, I'll ask an officer to get to you as quickly as possible.'

Ten minutes later, the Garda control centre gets the following message from the officer: 'Please disregard the distress call. His wife explained that the gentleman got into the back seat of his car by mistake.'

Beware of Wishes

Mary and Tommy were both 65 years old and were celebrating their forty-fifth wedding anniversary. After all the family and guests had gone, a fairy appeared from nowhere and said to them, 'Congratulations, you two. I'm here to grant you each one wish.'

Mary said, 'Oh, I've always wanted to travel around the world.'

The fairy waved her magic wand and ZING! – Mary had tickets in her hand for a first-class round-the-world cruise on a Cunard liner. Then the fairy asked Tommy what he wanted.

Tommy replied, 'I wish I had a wife thirty years younger than me.'

So the fairy waved her wand and ZING! – Tommy was 95 years old.

Too Trusting

Jacob is a very religious man. One day, a nearby river overflows its banks and floods the town, forcing Jacob and his wife to climb on to his garage roof. Soon, a man in a boat comes along and tells them to get in.

Jacob says, 'That's very kind of you, but no thanks. God will take care of us.' So, the boat leaves.

The water rises and Jacob and his wife have to climb on to the roof of his house. Another man in a boat comes along and tells Jacob to get in.

Jacob replies, 'That's very kind of you, but no thanks. God will take care of us.'

However, his wife decides she will take the offer and escapes in the boat.

The water rises further and soon Jacob is clinging to his chimney. Then a helicopter arrives and drops a ladder. The helicopter pilot tells Jacob to climb up the ladder.

Jacob replies, 'That's very kind of you, but no thanks. God will take care of me.'

The pilot says, 'Are you really sure?'

Jacob says, 'Yes, I'm sure that God will take care of me.'

Finally, the water rises too high and Jacob drowns. He goes up to Heaven and is met by God.

Jacob says to God, 'You told me you would take care of me. What happened?'

God replies, 'I sent you two boats and a helicopter. What else did you want me to do?'

I Wrote A Letter To My Love

A stupid Norwegian husband, masked in his own underpants, held up a bank. He presented a teller with a demand note and made off with the money. But he did not keep his ill-gotten gains long – his wife's name was written on the other side of the demand note.

The man claimed he didn't remember the robbery because he was drunk, but had thought the underpants looked familiar when he saw the photo of the robber in the paper, and he had found an unexplained wad of cash in his pocket . . .

Please Make Sure . . .

Two stupid husbands, George and Harry, are out hunting in the woods of New Jersey when Harry suddenly collapses. George rushes over to him, but he doesn't seem to be breathing and his eyes are glazed.

George is in a panic. He takes out his mobile phone, calls emergency services and shouts, 'Help, please help me! My friend Harry is dead! What on earth should I do?'

The operator tells George, 'Sir, please calm down. I can help you. First of all, let's make sure he's really dead.'

After a short silence, the operator hears a shot. Then George gets back on the phone. 'OK, now what?'

Too Focussed?

Wally drives his friend Jack to the shops. As they get out of the car, Wally locks the doors in such a hurry that he forgets to remove the ignition key first.

'Oh blast,' says Wally, 'I've done it again. Joanne is always telling me to be more careful.'

'Why don't we use a coat hanger to open the lock?' says Jack.

'No, we can't do that,' replies Wally, 'because people will think we're breaking into the car.'

'OK,' Jack suggests, We can use a penknife to cut the rubber seal around the quarter light, then I can reach in and get the key.'

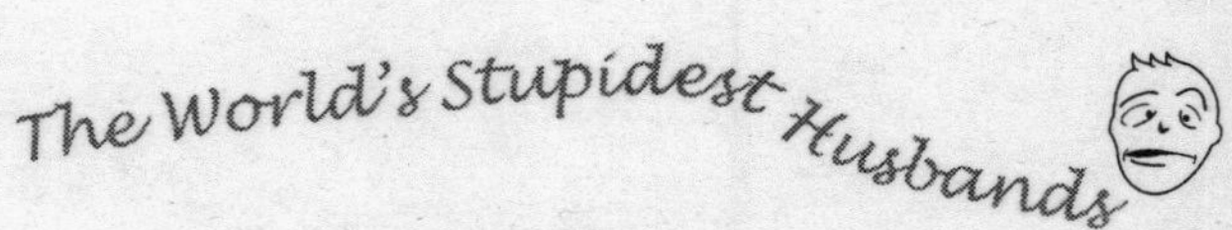

'No, absolutely not,' replies Wally. 'People will think we're stupid for not using a coat hanger.'

'Well,' says Jack, 'you'd better think of something quickly. It's starting to rain and your sun roof's still open.'

Shake It All About

A stupid husband was hard at work in his laboratory in Lafayette, Georgia, when a knock came on the front door. Because his work was rather illegal, he poured the two chemicals, red phosphorus and iodine, into an empty film container and stuffed it into his trouser pocket before opening the door. (The two chemicals are essential for making methamphetamine.)

Two social workers wanted him to fill out some forms, so he got into the back seat of their car and began writing.

'He kept fiddling with his front right pants pocket,' said the commander of the local Drug Task Force, according to the *Walker County Messenger*. The container was probably getting a bit hot by this point as the red phosphorus and

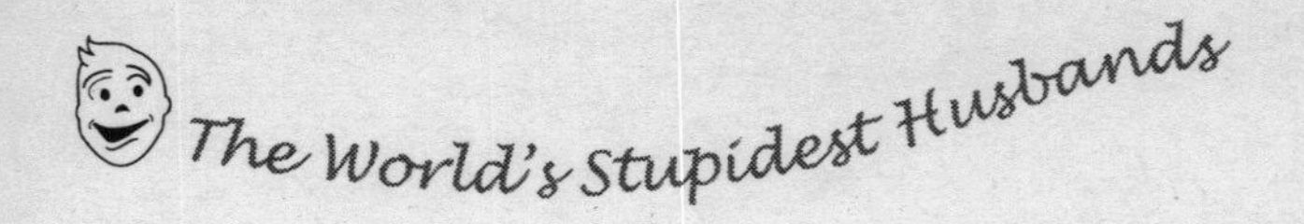

iodine mixed together, but the stupid husband was happy because his illegal activities were still secret. What he apparently did not know was that the mixture of red phosphorus and iodine would soon reach 137 °C (278 °F).

'All of a sudden, a loud bang happened, and fire shot from his pocket. It damaged the inside of the state vehicle and burned clothing on the case workers,' ran a later report on the incident.

The stupid husband suffered second- and third-degree burns to his testicles and leg. He was rushed to hospital, and shortly after he was hauled off to jail after the police raided the house and discovered his meth lab. He and his common-law wife were later charged with making and possessing illegal drugs.

Wipeout

At a Giants' baseball game in San Francisco, California, a 38-year-old surfer from Hawaii was leaning back against a railing, getting the last drops of a beer, when his expensive designer sunglasses slipped off the back of his head.

They landed 25 feet below, where a helpful man picked them up and tried to throw them back. But it was too far! The surfer called out that he was coming down to get them.

His wife described him as 'a passionate surfer' talented enough to turn pro, but his belief in his physical abilities was his downfall. Rather than make the long walk around and down to collect his sunglasses, he decided to climb over the rail, jump on to a light bracket 5 feet below, and then swing down to the ground.

At least, that was what the police assumed had been his plan. Unfortunately he missed the light bracket and 'came down like a pancake', according to a startled observer a few feet from where he landed.

The crowd was shocked into silence. Why would anyone take such a chance for a pair of sunglasses?

Would You Remarry?

'Dear,' asked a wife, 'What would you do if I died?'

'Heavens, darling, I would be extremely upset,' said the husband. 'Why?'

'Would you remarry?' persevered the wife.

'No, of course not, dear,' said the husband.

'Don't you like being married?'

'Of course I do, dear,' he said.

'Then why wouldn't you remarry?'

'All right,' said the husband, 'I'd remarry.'

'You would?' said the wife, looking hurt.

'Yes,' said the husband.

'Would you sleep with her in our bed?' asked the wife.

After a long pause. 'Well, yes, I suppose I would,' replied the husband.

'I see,' said the wife indignantly. 'And would you let her wear my old clothes?'

'I suppose, if she wanted to.'

'Really,' said the wife icily. 'And would you take down the pictures of me and replace them with pictures of her?'

'Yes. That would be the right thing to do.'

'And I suppose you'd let her play with my golf clubs, too!' said the wife in fury.

'Of course not, dear,' said the stupid husband. 'She's left-handed.'

Snap, Click, Boom!

A stupid husband from Brazil was employed to clean out the carrying tanks of petrol tankers. He had been in the job for two months when his stupidity caught up with him.

He had begun to fill a tanker with water, so that any flammable vapour would be forced out of the carrying tank. He returned an hour later to check whether the water level was high enough for him to proceed. However, because it was dark inside the tanker, he couldn't decide if there was enough water inside.

Using his initiative, if not his intelligence, he lit a cigarette lighter to check the water level. The result successfully proved that the water level was not high enough because the subsequent explosion tossed him into the company car park over 300 feet away.

Our stupid Brazilian suffered severe burns and a head injury which exposed his brain. By the time the firemen and paramedics arrived he had died, leaving a wife and four children with no means of support.

Driving On Ice

Ignoring all warnings, one stupid husband drove his pickup truck on to the icy surface of Saginaw Bay, Michigan. Predictably, the vehicle broke through the ice, but the man managed to escape from the sinking truck. He reached the shore wet, cold, but alive.

Despite his traumatic experience, and despite a day of sunshine and warm temperatures, the man returned to Saginaw Bay late the following night. This time he was driving an all-terrain vehicle, and accompanied by a friend. Again the vehicle plunged through the ice.

The friend survived, but the stupid husband had used up his luck. His body was later recovered by the Coast Guard many miles away.

Jacks Away

A stupid husband from New Zealand had to make repairs underneath his car. However, when he jacked the car up, he couldn't get underneath. So he removed the battery from the boot, positioned the jack on top of it, and pumped up the jack. Then he crawled underneath to repair his car with plenty of space to spare.

Unfortunately, car batteries are not designed to carry that much weight. The battery collapsed and the jack slipped, trapping him beneath the car. Unable to breathe because of the weight on his chest, he died in a pool of battery acid.

The terrifying thing is that he was employed as a accident prevention officer at a large food-processing factory. Worse, ten years earlier, he had been working under a car when the jack had collapsed, trapping him and breaking one of his legs.

How can you tell which computer your stupid husband has been using?

There's Tippex all over the screen.

My Loving Wife

A stupid husband caught the flu and was forced to stay in bed. He was glad for the respite, because it taught him how much his wife loved him.

He told his friends later she was so thrilled to have him around that, whenever a delivery man or the mailman arrived, she ran out and yelled, 'My husband's home! My husband's home!'

A Fishy Problem

Two stupid husbands are out fishing and they are having really good luck. They are catching fish so fast they have to stop early.

'This is great,' says the first husband. 'We should mark the spot so we can come here again.'

'You're right,' says the other husband, who then dives over the side and paints a big X on the bottom of the boat.

They head back to land and, just as they're about to dock, the first husband looks at the second and says, 'But what if we don't get the same boat next time?'

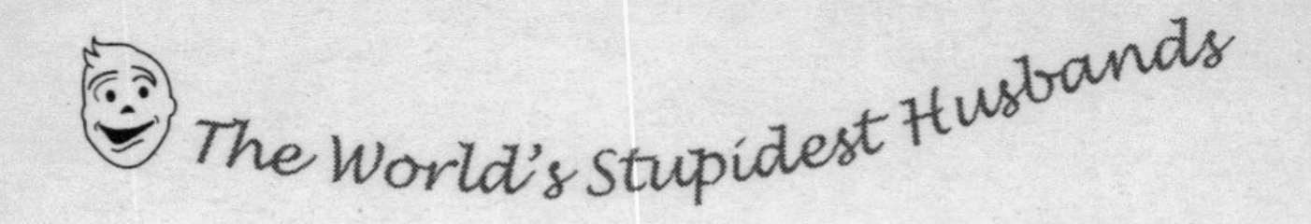

The Code Of The Hunter

Two stupid husbands go hunting. Soon they get separated and, as happens, one mistakes the other for a deer and shoots him.

After much effort he drags his friend out of the woods, throws him into the 4x4 and drives him to the nearest hospital.

'Will he be all right?' the worried hunter asks the doctor.

'It's hard to say,' says the doctor. 'But he'd have had a better chance if you hadn't gutted and skinned him.'

Who Makes The Coffee?

A stupid husband and his wife were having an argument about who should make the coffee each morning.

The wife said, 'You should do it, because you get up first.'

The husband said, 'You are in charge of the cooking, so you should do it because that is your job. I can wait for my coffee.'

The wife replied, 'No, you should do it. And besides, the Bible says that the man should make the coffee.'

The stupid husband replies, 'I don't believe that, show me.'

So she fetched a Bible, opened it at the New Testament, and showed him at the top of several pages, that it does indeed say: 'HEBREWS'.

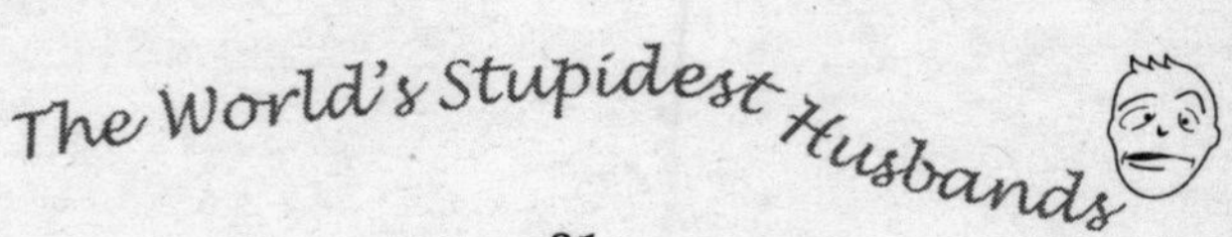

Going Out With A Bang

The 4th of July is Independence Day in the United States of America and the celebrations usually include a festival of fireworks.

In 2000, a stupid husband from New York was partially beheaded while peering into a launching tube at an Independence Day party.

The firework concerned was supposed to be the grand finale and, in his haste to get it working, he put his head right over the mouth of the tube. As he did so, the firework went off, giving the party an unexpected – yet gorily spectacular – finish.

My Husband Is SOOOO Stupid . . .

. . . he went to the 24-hour supermarket and asked what time they closed.

. . . he asked for a refund on a jigsaw puzzle because he said it was broken.

. . . he asked me what the number for 999 was.

. . . he could trip over a cordless phone.

. . . when he filled out a job application that asked 'Race?', he wrote 'Grand National'.

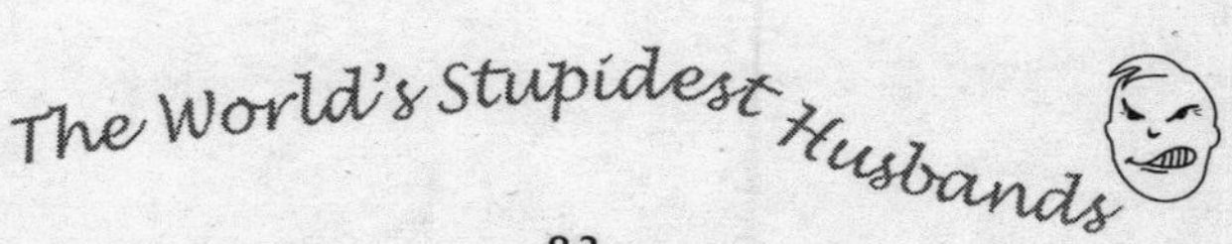

My Husband Is SOOOO Stupid . . .

. . . he got locked *in* his car.

. . . he stared at a can of juice for three hours because it said 'concentrate'.

. . . he lost his shadow.

. . . he makes Homer Simpson look like a Nobel Prize winner.

. . . he sent me a fax with a 1st class stamp on it.

Falls Off Niagara

In October 1995, a stupid husband equipped himself with a homemade rocket-parachute contraption and rode a jet ski over the Canadian side of Niagara Falls at full throttle.

His plan was that the rocket would propel him clear of the falls, then the parachute would float him down to the river below, where he would be fished out by the *Maid o' the Mist* tour boat.

Regrettably, the rocket failed to ignite and the parachute failed to open. However, according to plan, his body was recovered from the river by the *Maid o' the Mist* crew.

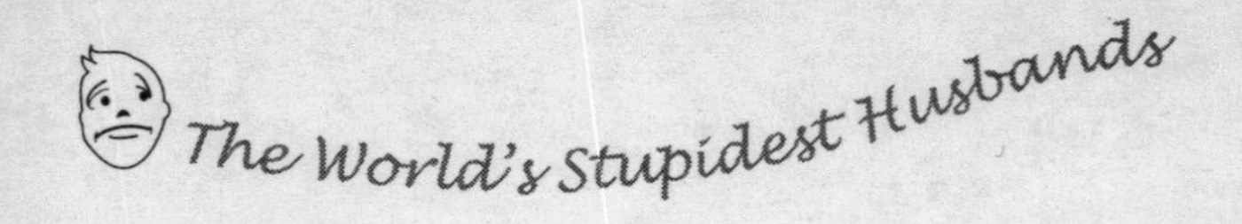

Inside? Outside?

A British construction firm was fined a six-figure sum after the deaths of two workers in London.

The two men, both married and reportedly experienced in their work, fell 100 feet after drilling a hole through thick concrete without realizing they were standing in the centre of the circle. Neither was wearing a safety harness.

A Glutton For Punishment

In 2001, a resident of Philadelphia, USA, wondered what it felt like to be hit by a bullet . . . so he took a gun and shot himself in the shoulder. For the second time, emergency services rushed to his home to treat a gunshot wound.

Why did he shoot himself, not once but twice? His wife said that he wanted to see if it hurt as much as it did the first time . . .

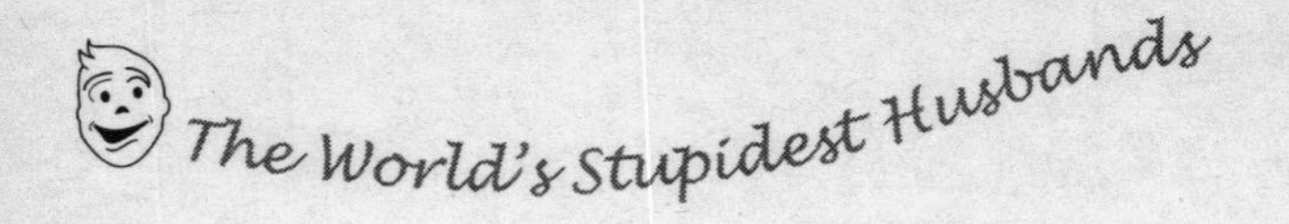

What's Your Position?

Edward and his wife Sally are out sailing in his expensive yacht when he gets into difficulties and has to call out the lifeboat.

Because the coastguard needs an accurate fix on the yacht's location, he calls the yacht on the radio. 'What is your position?' he asks, 'Repeat, what is your position?'

Edward replies, 'Oh, I've just been promoted. I'm marketing director of the second-largest advertising agency in Britain!'

Double Trouble

Samuel goes with Sarah to his local opticians to buy a new pair of glasses for himself. He chooses a pair 'off-the shelf', pays for them and leaves wearing them.

As they are a bit hungry, they decide to have a coffee and a sandwich at a nearby restaurant.

While he is looking through the menu, Samuel says, 'Sarah, you better order for me. I'm seeing everything double with my new glasses. And while you're doing that, I'm going to the toilet.'

When Samuel returns, Sarah notices that the front of his trousers are wet.

'Oy vay,' says Sarah, 'what happened, Samuel? Your trousers are all wet!'

'You wouldn't believe it,' Samuel replies, 'I was standing in front of the urinal and when I looked down, I saw two. So I put one back!'

Snow Warnings

Fred is married to Sandra, and they live in Chelmsford. One very cold winter morning, they hear the following local radio announcement: 'We're expecting up to 3 inches of snow today. To help the gritting lorries get through, please park your car on the even-numbered side of your street.'

So Fred goes out and moves the car.

The following morning, they hear another snow warning on the radio: 'We're expecting another 4 inches of snow today. To help the gritting lorries get through, please park your car on the odd-numbered side of your street.'

Fred goes out and moves the car again.

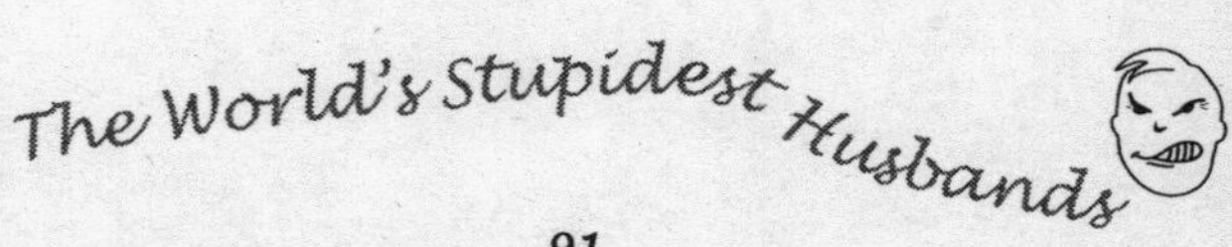

The next morning, they hear yet another snow warning on the radio, 'We're expecting a blizzard today – at least another 6 inches of snow. You must park . . . ' when suddenly there is a power cut and the radio goes dead.

Fred says to Sandra, 'Darling, now I don't know what to do. What do you think I should do?'

Sandra replies, 'Well, darling, why not just leave the car in our heated garage this time?'

Stupid Things Stupid Men Say

I haven't committed a crime. What I did was fail to comply with the law.

DAVID DINKINS, EX-MAYOR OF NEW YORK CITY, IN RESPONSE TO ACCUSATIONS THAT HE HAD FAILED TO PAY HIS TAXES.

We're going to turn this team around 360 degrees.

JASON KIDD, ON BEING DRAFTED TO THE DALLAS MAVERICKS

'Hawaii is a unique state. It is a small state. It is a state that is by itself. It is different from the other forty-nine states. Well, all states are different, but it's got a particularly unique situation.

DAN QUAYLE, FORMER US VICE-PRESIDENT

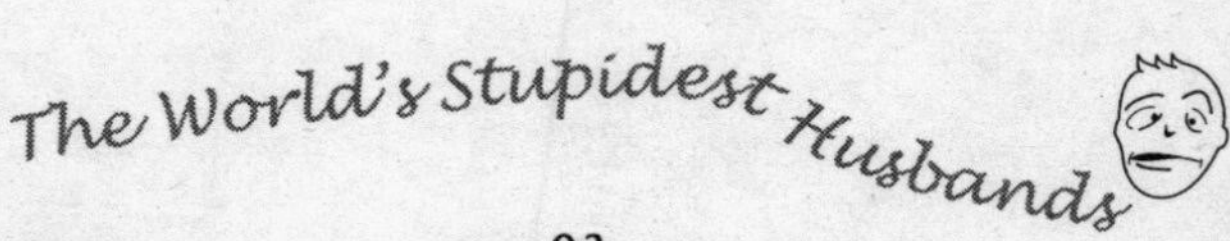

Stupid Things Stupid Men Say

China is a big country, inhabited by many Chinese.

CHARLES DE GAULLE, FORMER FRENCH PRESIDENT

Half this game is 90 per cent mental.

DANNY OZARK, PHILADELPHIA PHILLIES MANAGER

Outside of the killings, Washington has one of the lowest crime rates in the country.

EX-MAYOR MARION BARRY, WASHINGTON DC, DEFENDING HIS RECORD ON LAW AND ORDER

Am I Legless?

Stephen had been drinking at a pub all night. The bartender finally said that the bar was closing. So Stephen stood up to leave and fell flat on his face. He tried to stand one more time; same result. Stephen decided to crawl outside and get some fresh air – maybe that would sober him up.

Once outside, Stephen stood up, but fell flat on his face again. So he decided to crawl the three blocks to his home. When he arrived at the door, Stephen stood up and again fell flat on his face.

He crawled through the door, upstairs and into his bedroom. When he reached his bed, Stephen tried once more to stand up. This time he managed to pull himself upright, but he quickly

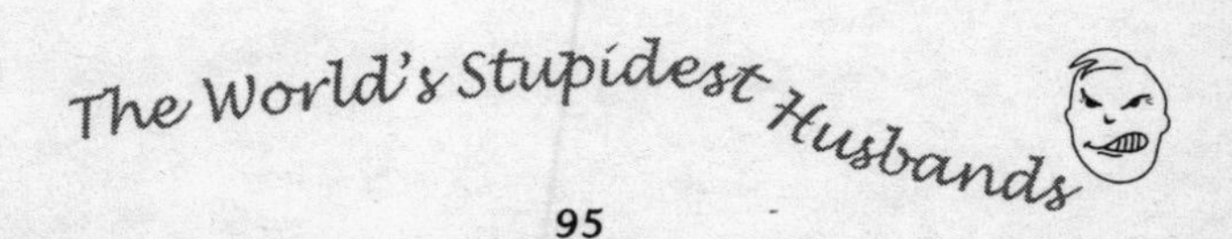

fell right into bed and fell sound asleep as soon as his head hit the pillow.

He was awakened the next morning by his wife, Mary, shouting, 'You've been out getting drunk again!'

'Whatever makes you think that?' Stephen asked, putting on an innocent look.

Mary replied 'The pub called – you've left your wheelchair there again.'

Stand In Line

The end of the world has come. God looks over the millions and millions of people and says to them: 'Welcome to Heaven. I want the women to go with St Peter. Go now and follow him. And you men, I want you to form two lines. The first line, to the left of me, is for men who dominated their women on earth. The second line, to the right of me, is for men who were dominated by their women. OK, now line up.'

There was much movement for some length of time, but eventually the women are gone and there are two lines of men. The line of the men that were dominated by their women is 150 miles long. The line of men that dominated women has only one man.

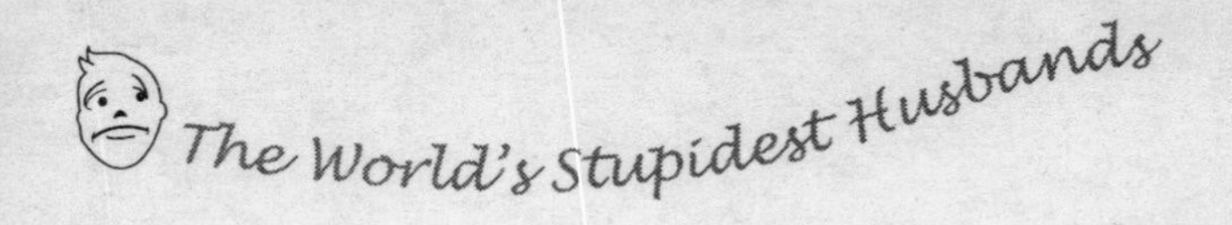

God is angry and says, 'You men should be ashamed of yourselves. I created you in my image and yet you were all dominated by your mates. Look at the only one of my sons that stood up and made me proud. Learn from him!'

He turns to the man and says, 'Tell them, my son. How did you manage to be the only one on that line?'

The man says, 'I don't know, my wife told me to stand here.'

Stupid Things Stupid Men Say

And now, will y'all stand and be recognized?

GIB LEWIS, TEXAS SPEAKER OF THE HOUSE,
TO A DISABLED AUDIENCE ON DISABILITY DAY

Nature intended women to be our slaves . . . they are our property; we are not theirs. They belong to us, just as a tree that bears fruit belongs to a gardener. What a mad idea to demand equality for women! Women are nothing but machines for producing children.

NAPOLEON BONAPARTE,
FIRST CONSUL AND EMPEROR OF FRANCE

Stupid Things Stupid Men Say

The meaning of woman is to be meaningless. She represents negation, the opposite pole from the Godhead, the other possibility of humanity.

OTTO WEININGER,
AUSTRIAN PHILOSOPHER

'Literature cannot be the business of a woman's life, and it ought not to be. The more she is engaged in her proper duties, the less leisure will she have for it, even as an accomplishment and a recreation.'

ROBERT SOUTHEY,
BRITISH POET

Hoist By His Own Petard

A retired Belgian engineer booby-trapped his home, intending to kill his estranged family, but died after he was accidentally killed by one of his own devices.

At first, police assumed that the 79-year-old had committed suicide, because he was found alone with a bullet wound in his neck.

Then a detective missed death by inches when he opened a booby-trapped wooden chest. The police retreated hastily and called in military experts.

The experts took three weeks to decipher nineteen of an enigmatic series of clues, but were forced to admit defeat on the twentieth. They located concealed shotguns triggered by

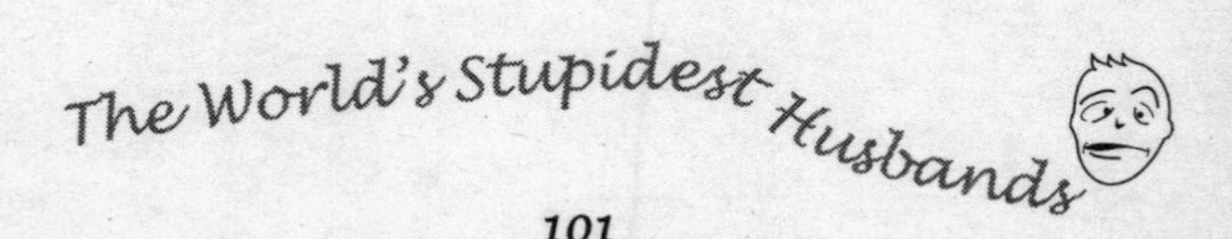

threads in walls and ceilings. Other traps included a crate of beer set to explode after a certain number of bottles were removed.

Neighbours described him as a taciturn but harmless man who enjoyed working in his garage. But relatives said he never forgave his wife for divorcing him twenty years earlier.

Police believe that he began installing the traps after losing a lengthy battle to keep his home, and guessed that the notes were intended to assist his failing memory . . .

Engage Brain First?

One stupid husband drowned in a lake in Ontario province, Canada, in 2002. It was a very hot July weekend when this man took his family for a boat ride. However, the breeze out on the lake did not cool him off enough, so he turned off the boat's engine and dived into the lake.

Now, this is risky. During the summer, a thin surface layer of warmer water covers the colder depths. You can be paralyzed when you hit the cold water a few feet below the surface. But this stupid husband didn't get that deep – he couldn't swim, and none of the family was wearing a life jacket.

Because he had dived off the upwind side of the boat, the wind pushed the boat away from him. It also stopped his wife throwing him a life preserver.

Even worse, he had failed to show his wife how to use the boat, so she could not start the engine and rescue him.

Although his family in the boat waved and shouted to the shore to try to get help, they were unable to attract anyone's attention because the boat had none of the usual safety aids, even a whistle.

Lifeguards, who recovered the body later, described the entire trip as an accident waiting to happen.

Stupid Things Stupid Men Say

I've read about foreign policy and studied – I know the number of continents.

GOVERNOR GEORGE WALLACE, DURING THE 1968 US PRESIDENTIAL CAMPAIGN

Traditionally, most of Australia's imports come from overseas.

KEPPEL ENDERBERY, FORMER AUSTRALIAN CABINET MINISTER

The people in the Navy look on motherhood as being compatible with being a woman.

REAR ADMIRAL JAMES R. HOGG

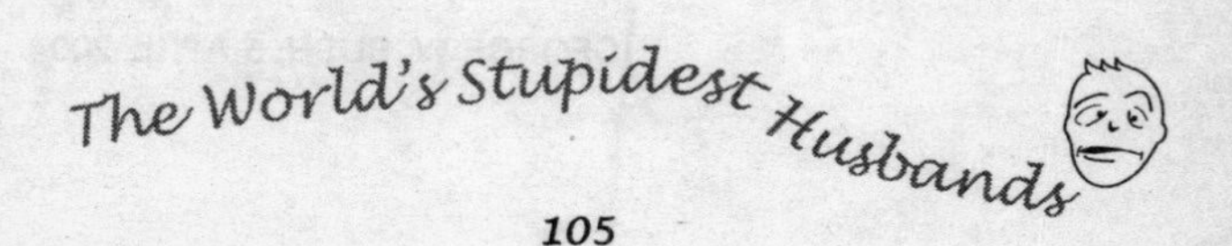

Stupid Things Stupid Men Say

Who could have possibly envisioned an erection – an election in Iraq at this point in history?

GEORGE W. BUSH, US PRESIDENT, 10 JANUARY 2005

I cut the taxes on everybody. I didn't cut them. The Congress cut them. I asked them to cut them.

GEORGE W. BUSH, 6 AUGUST 2004

We're still being challenged in Iraq and the reason why is a free Iraq will be a major defeat in the cause of freedom.

GEORGE W. BUSH, 5 APRIL 2004

When First We Practice To Deceive

In March 2002 in Ohio, a police chief radioed his headquarters to report that he'd been shot in the leg during an incident.

He said that he had pulled over a rusted Chevrolet without its licence plates, but before he could get out of his car, the driver had opened fire and put a bullet through the police car's windscreen. The driver then attacked the police chief, who was shot in the leg during the struggle. The police naturally launched a state-wide manhunt to find the gunman.

One week later, the law enforcement team nabbed their man: the police chief himself, who confessed to making up the entire incident.

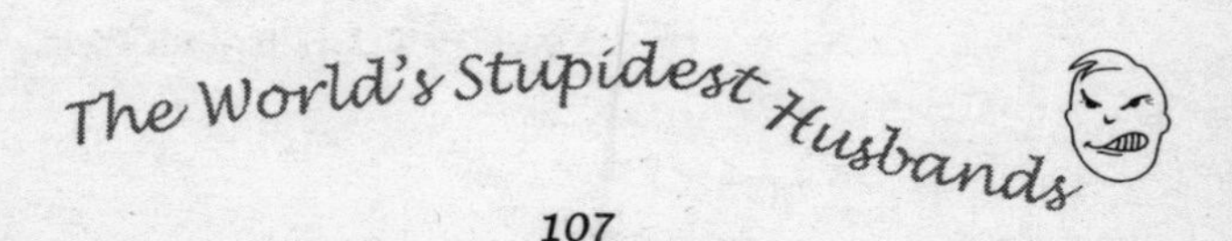

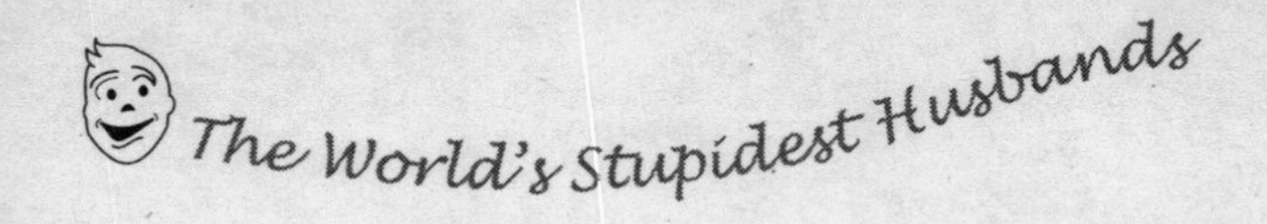

It started when he had accidentally fired his rifle through the windscreen of his police car.

To cover up that mistake, he had driven out to a county road, radioed in for help, and fired his gun to make it sound like there was trouble at the scene of a traffic stop.

Then he accidentally fired his gun again . . . and hit himself in the leg. Apparently he is no longer a member of the Ohio police . . .

Tally-ho!

A pilot and his passenger were hunting coyotes from the air in Montana, USA, when the passenger accidentally fired his shotgun into the right wing of the aircraft, causing the plane to crash.

The two hunters were injured, but survived, as did the fortunate coyote.

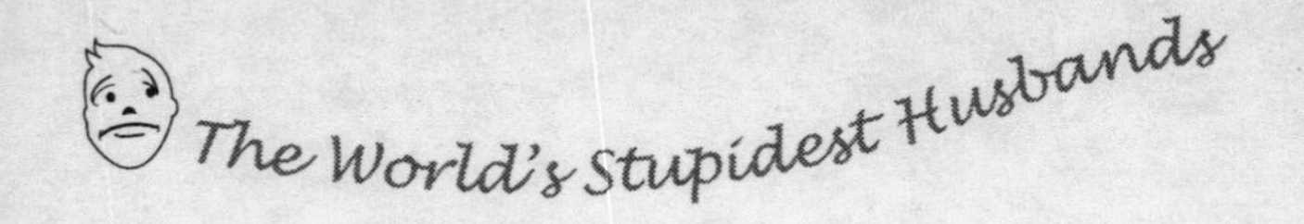

Simple Arithmetic

At a reservoir near Castlemaine in central Victoria, Australia, a group of stupid husbands set out to shoot duck. They were using a small aluminium dinghy, which was only warranted to carry three adults. In fact it was carrying the four friends from Melbourne, the son of one of them, six shotguns, and three crates of ammo. The total load was over 500 kg (1,100 lb).

There was no room for life jackets, so they were left behind. All the men were wearing waders, which act like lead weights if filled with water. It is virtually impossible to swim wearing them.

Hardly surprisingly, the boat capsized a thousand feet from shore, pitching everyone into the water. Two of the men were rescued by other boats, but father, son and another man were found dead.

Don't Believe Everything You See

A man and his wife have been stranded on a deserted island for many years. One morning, after a bad storm, another man (named Joe) washes up on the shore. Joe and the wife fancy each other at once, but realize they need to be careful.

The husband, however, is very glad to see Joe there. 'Now we can have three people doing an 8-hour shift in the watchtower, rather than two people doing a 12-hour shift,' he said.

Joe volunteers to take the first shift. He climbs up the tower and stands watch, searching the horizon for any ships. Soon the husband and wife start making a fire place to cook supper. Joe yells down, 'Hey, no fucking!'

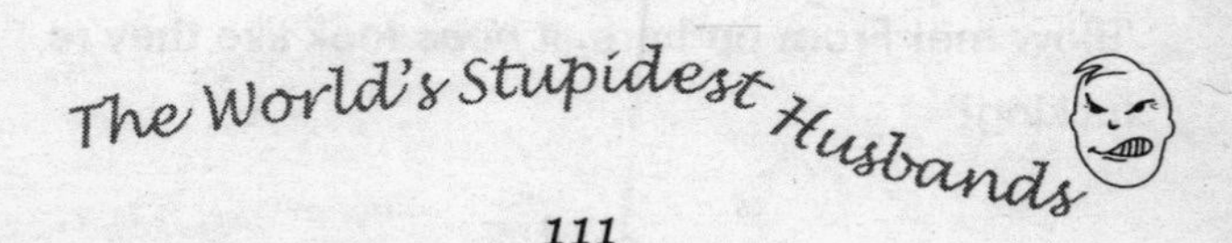

The couple look at each other and yell back: 'We're not fucking!'

A few minutes later they start to put driftwood into the stone circle. Again Joe yells down, 'Heeey, no fucking!'

Again they yell back, 'We're not fucking!'

Later they are patching the roof of their shack with palm leaves. Once again Joe yells down from high above, 'Hey, I said no fucking!!'

'We said we're not fucking!!' they reply.

Finally his shift is over. Joe climbs down and the husband starts to climb up. He's only halfway up when the wife and Joe are at it like rabbits.

At the top, the husband looks down and says, 'Blow me! From up here, it *does* look like they're fucking!'

He Could Have Put It Better

A man staggers into an emergency room with concussion, multiple bruises, two black eyes and a five iron wrapped tightly around his throat.

Naturally, the doctor asks him what happened.

'Well, it was like this,' said the man. 'I was having a quiet round of golf with my wife. At a difficult hole, we both sliced our balls into a field of cows.

'We went to look for the balls and, while I was rooting around, I noticed one of the cows had something white at its rear end. I walked over and lifted up the tail, and sure enough, there was

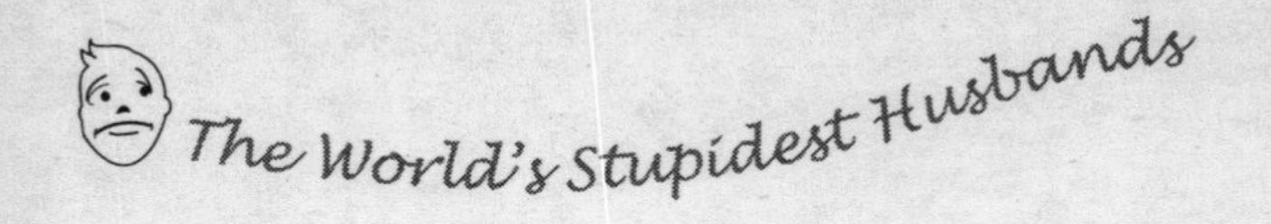

a golf ball with my wife's monogram on it – stuck right in the middle of the cow's bum.

'And that's when I made my big mistake.'

'What did you do?' asks the doctor.

'Well, I lifted the cow's tail again and yelled to my wife, "Hey, this looks like yours!" I don't remember much after that!'

Ear Ache

Following an argument with his wife about whether the train was coming or not, a Romanian man placed his ear against the rail to listen for the arrival of a train scheduled to stop at their station.

Instead, the 46-year-old man was hit by an express train coming the other way, and died instantly from head injuries.

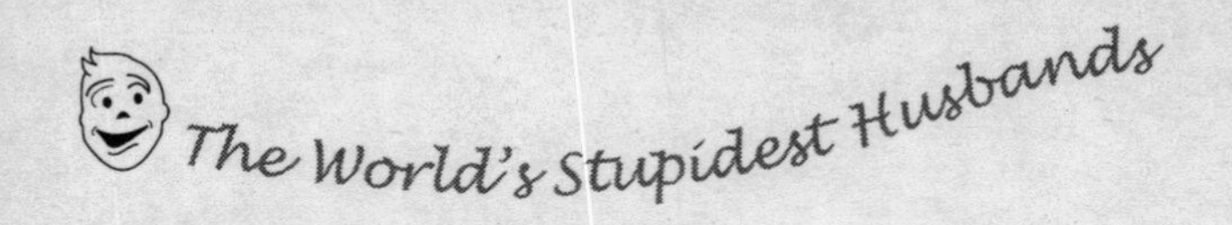

How do you know your husband is faithful?

The alimony cheques arrive on time.

ꙮ

My husband died at sea.
He would have sent out an SOS,
but he couldn't spell it.

My Husband Is SOOOO Stupid . . .

. . . he thought root beer was beer you could plant.

. . . he thought that intercourse was a racetrack.

. . . I told him the drinks were on the house, so he went and got a ladder.

. . . he thought that *coq au vin* was sex in a truck.

. . . he thought that genitalia was the name of an Italian airline.

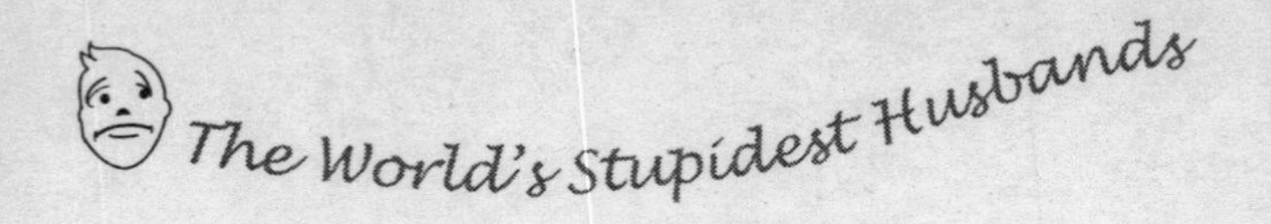

My Husband Is SOOOO Stupid . . .

. . . he thought that fellatio was a character in *Hamlet.*

. . . he took a ruler to bed to see how long he slept.

. . . he took toilet paper to a crap game.

. . . he tried to drown a fish.

. . . he thought that Shirley Temple was a children's synagogue.

Balling a Bear

A 41-year-old Dutchman visited an Amsterdam zoo, and at the bear enclosure asked whether the bear was a male or female. Nobody knew, so he decided to find out.

He climbed the 7-foot fence and jumped into the enclosure. Despite urgent warnings from the crowd, he approached the 390-pound adult, which was quietly playing with a ball, and unaware of the intruder. Amazingly, the man was able to take a look at its anatomy, but could not form a judgement as to its sex. So he delivered a good, hard kick between its legs.

The bear turned out to be a male, and responded to the assault in a typical male bear fashion. He roared in pain, and charged towards the Dutchman, who attempted to defend himself

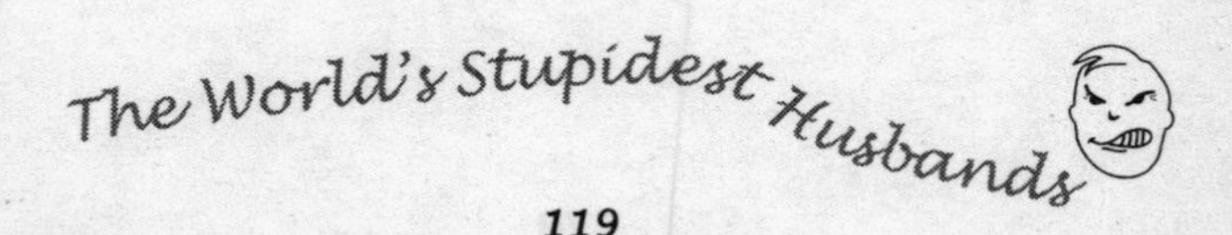

with a hasty karate kick while he ran for the fence. This brilliant defence tactic failed completely, and the bear mauled him to death. Zoo keepers arrived, but not soon enough to save his life.

No one could discover why the man had done what he did. There were no drugs or alcohol in his system, and his wife reported that he was not suicidal, nor did they know of any mental defects other than 'an exaggerated sense of bravado'.

Apart from a pair of badly swollen testicles, the bear was uninjured.

Stupid Is, Stupid Does

'I never would have married you if I knew how stupid you were,' shouted the woman at her husband.

He replied, 'You should've known how stupid I was the minute I asked you to marry me.'

Weighly Misguided

A husband stepped on one of those coin-operated scales that tell you your fortune and weight, and dropped in a coin.

'Listen to this,' he said to his wife, showing her a small, white card. 'It says I'm energetic, bright, resourceful and a great lover.'

'Yeah,' his wife nodded, 'and it has your weight wrong, too.'

A Man's Perspective

One night a wife found her husband standing over their newborn baby's cot. Silently she watched him.

As he stood looking down at the sleeping infant, she saw on his face a mixture of emotions: disbelief, doubt, delight, amazement, enchantment, scepticism. Touched by this unusual display and the deep emotions it aroused, with eyes glistening she slipped her arms around her husband.

'A penny for your thoughts,' she whispered in his ear.

'It's amazing!' he replied. 'I just can't see how anybody can make a cot like that for only £29.99!'

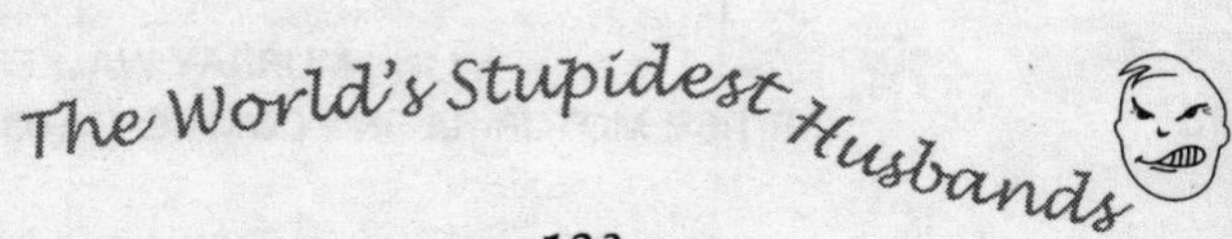

Stupid Sports Moments

Ian Botham walked out to bat during England's tour of Western Australia in 1986–7. He had reached the crease and was awaiting the first ball, when the twelfth man panted up and handed over an essential piece of equipment – his bat!

'My sister's expecting a baby, and I don't know if I'm going to be an uncle or an aunt.'

CHUCK NEVITT, NORTH CAROLINA STATE BASKETBALL PLAYER, EXPLAINING WHY HE APPEARED NERVOUS AT PRACTICE

'The lead car is absolutely unique, except for the one behind it which is identical.'

MURRAY WALKER, BRITISH MOTOR-RACING COMMENTATOR

After a quarrel, a husband said
to his wife, 'You know, I was a
fool when I married you.'

The wife replied, 'Yes, dear,
but I was in love and didn't notice.'

What do you call a man who has
lost 99 per cent of his brain?

A widower.

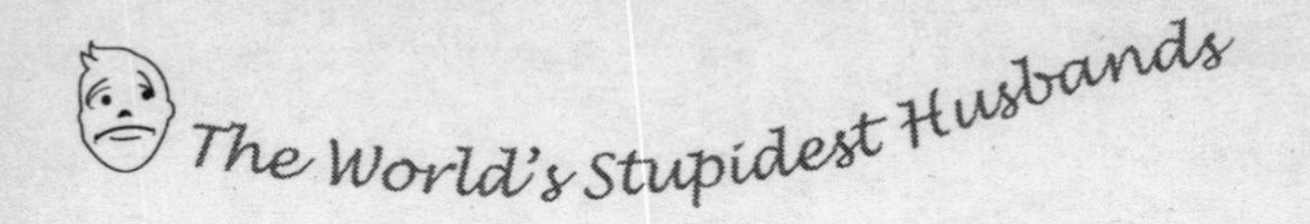

The Goody Bag

God had just about finished creating the universe, but He had a couple of leftover things in his bag of creations, so He stopped by to visit Adam and Eve in the Garden of Eden.

One of the things He had to give away was the ability to stand up and pee.

'It's a very handy thing,' God told the couple, whom He found hanging around under an apple tree. 'I was wondering if either one of you wanted that ability.'

Adam jumped up and begged, 'Oh, give that to me! I'd love to be able to do that! It seems the sort of thing a man should do. Oh please, oh please, oh please, let me have that ability. It'd be so great! When I'm working in the garden or naming the animals, I could just let it rip. It'd be so cool! Oh please, God, let it be me to whom you give that gift, let me stand and pee, oh please . . .'

Eve just smiled and shook her head at the display. She told God that if Adam really wanted it so badly – and it certainly seemed to be the sort of thing that would make him happy – she really wouldn't mind if Adam were the one given the ability to stand up and pee.

And so it was. And it was . . . well, good.

'Fine,' God said, looking back into the bag at the last of His leftover gifts. 'What else is there? Oh yes, multiple orgasms . . .'

Michael O'Mara Humour

All Michael O'Mara titles are available by post from:
Bookpost, PO Box 29, Douglas, Isle of Man, IM99 1BQ

Credit cards accepted. Telephone: 01624 677237 Fax: 01624 670923
Email: bookshop@enterprise.net Internet: www.bookpost.co.uk

Free postage and packing in the UK.

Other Michael O'Mara Humour titles include:

The Book of Urban Legends............................ISBN 1-85479-932-0 pb £3.99
Born for the Job ....ISBN 1-84317-099-X pb £5.99
The Complete Book of Farting ....ISBN 1-85479-440-X pb £4.99
The Ultimate Insult..ISBN 1-85479-288-1 pb £5.99
Wicked Cockney Rhyming Slang ....ISBN 1-85479-386-1 pb £3.99
The Wicked Wit of Jane Austen ....ISBN 1-85479-652-6 hb £9.99
The Wicked Wit of Winston Churchill.............ISBN 1-85479-529-5 hb £9.99
The Wicked Wit of Oscar Wilde ....ISBN 1-85479-542-2 hb £9.99
The World's Stupidest Laws ....ISBN 1-84317-172-4 pb £4.99
The World's Stupidest Signs...........................ISBN 1-84317-170-8 pb £4.99
More of the World's Stupidest Signs..............ISBN 1-84317-032-9 pb £4.99
The World's Stupidest Last Words ....ISBN 1-84317-021-3 pb £4.99
The World's Stupidest Inventions ....ISBN 1-84317-036-1 pb £5.99
The World's Stupidest Instructions ....ISBN 1-84317-078-7 pb £4.99
The World's Stupidest Sporting Screw-Ups....ISBN 1-84317-039-6 pb £4.99
The World's Stupidest Chat-Up Lines ....ISBN 1-84317-019-1 pb £4.99
The World's Stupidest Headlines....................ISBN 1-84317-105-8 pb £4.99
The World's Stupidest Celebrities...................ISBN 1-84317-137-6 pb £4.99
The World's Stupidest Deaths ....ISBN 1-84317-136-8 pb £4.99
Cricket: It's A Funny Old Game ....ISBN 1-84317-090-6 pb £4.99
Football: It's A Funny Old Game......................ISBN 1-84317-091-4 pb £4.99
Laughable Latin..ISBN 1-84317-097-3 pb £4.99
School Rules...ISBN 1-84317-100-7 pb £4.99
Sex Cheques (new edition) ....ISBN 1-84317-121-X pb £3.50
The Timewaster Letters ....ISBN 1-84317-108-2 pb £9.99
The Jordan Joke Book......................................ISBN 1-84317-120-1 pb £4.99
Speak Well English ....ISBN 1-84317-088-4 pb £5.99
Shite's Unoriginal Miscellany ....ISBN 1-84317-064-7 hb £9.99
Eats, Shites & Leaves ....ISBN 1-84317-098-1 hb £9.99
A Shite History of Nearly Everything..............ISBN 1-84317-138-4 hb £9.99